The MAILBOX®
The Education Center®

Sort All Sorts

115 Picture- and Word- Categorizing Activities

- ★ **Literacy Sorts**
- ★ **Math Sorts**
- ★ **Science Sorts**
- ★ **Social Studies Sorts**

Managing Editor: Lynn Drolet

Editorial Team: Becky S. Andrews, Diane Badden, Kimberley Bruck, Karen A. Brudnak, Pam Crane, Sarah Foreman, Tazmen Hansen, Marsha Heim, Lori Z. Henry, Debra Liverman, Kitty Lowrance, Jennifer Nunn, Tina Petersen, Mark Rainey, Greg D. Rieves, Hope Rodgers, Donna K. Teal, Rachael Traylor, Sharon M. Tresino, Zane Williard

Plus tips and tools for sorting!

www.themailbox.com

©2010 The Mailbox® Books
All rights reserved.
ISBN10 #1-56234-949-X • ISBN13 #978-1-56234-949-3

Printed in the United States
10 9 8 7 6 5 4 3 2 1

HPS 215492

Table of Contents

Math Sorts

Number Sense

Comparing Numbers

Addition

Subtraction

Addition and Subtraction

Odd and Even Numbers

Geometry

Fractions

Measurement

Time

Money

Science Sorts

Social Studies Sorts

Sorting Tools

Programmable Sorts

Recording Sheets

Storage

What's

Sort 43: Digraphs

shell	fish

Picture Sorts

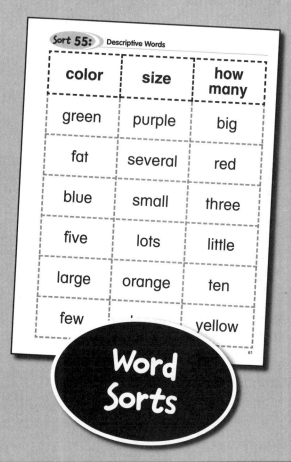

Sort 55: Descriptive Words

color	size	how many
green	purple	big
fat	several	red
blue	small	three
five	lots	little
large	orange	ten
few		yellow

Word Sorts

Sorts for...

Literacy

Math

Science

Social Studies

INSIDE

Sort 16: Short-Vowel and Long-Vowel Word Families

cat	hay	no match
tray	hat	play
rat	pay	bat
spray	mat	rake

Picture and Word Sorts

Programmable Sort:

Programmable Sorts

Recording Sheet Name:

Recording Sheets

Handy Tips
See page 6.

Storage

Handy Sorting Tips

For ready-to-use recording sheets, make a back-to-back copy of pages 126 and 127 for each child. Laminate the copies and store them with a class supply of wipe-off markers.

For a quick center activity, put a laminated sort inside a gift bag.

For easy identification, have students glue each category card on a slightly larger construction paper rectangle.

Use the handy envelope pattern on page 128 to make storage envelopes. Additional storage options include business-size envelopes, resealable plastic bags, and string-tie envelopes.

Copy sorts onto colorful paper for added interest. Or use colorful paper to color-code sorts by curriculum area. For example, use white for literacy, yellow for math, green for science, and blue for social studies.

Use a variety of sorting activities, such as the following:

Closed sort: A student sorts the cards into the provided categories.

Open sort: Category cards are removed. A student looks for similarities among his cards and sorts them accordingly. Because open sorts often result in a variety of outcomes, allow time for students to explain their sorts.

Partner sort: A student works with a partner to complete an open or a closed sort.

Blind sort: For this auditory sort, display the category cards. Then name each of the remaining picture or word cards. Have students point to, name, or signal the appropriate category for each card.

Speed sort: This is a timed closed sort. Over several days, a student works to decrease the amount of time it takes to accurately complete a sort. This type of sort promotes speed with accuracy and should only be used to encourage automatic recognition.

Sort 1: Rhyming

 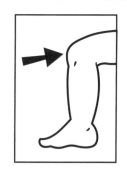 

 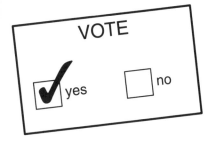 

VOTE

☑ yes ☐ no

Sort 2: Rhyming

  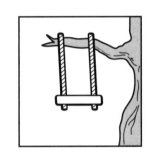

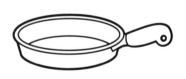 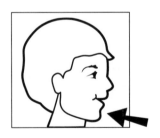 

Sorts of All Sorts • ©The Mailbox® Books • TEC61267

1		2
		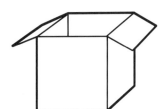

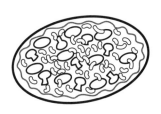		

1	2	3

		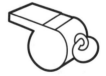

bell 	mop 	sun

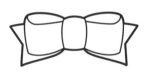		
		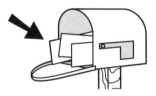

gum	nest	pot 

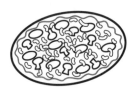		
		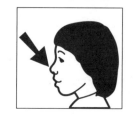

Final Consonants

drum 	bus 	cat 

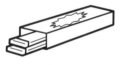		

han**d**	sea**l** 	jee**p**

mop

hen

hop

pen

ten

drop

men

top

Note to the teacher: Have a student sort the pictures and words; then have her match each word to its picture.

map 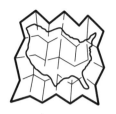   **bag**

tag   nap   wag

clap   lap   flag

Note to the teacher: Have a student sort the pictures and words; then have her match each word to its picture.

h**at**	c**an**	no match

van	mat	man
cat	pan	sad
rat	fan	bat

Note to the teacher: Have a student sort the pictures and words; then have her match each word to its picture.

pig	hit	lip
sit	dip	fig
zip	pit	slip
kit	big	fit
twig	sip	rig
rip	skit	wig
bit	dig	trip

mug   **dog**   **pot**

jog	hot	bug
hug	rug	log
cot	frog	dot

Note to the teacher: Have a student sort the pictures and words; then have her match each word to its picture.

back 	sock	duck 
tuck	dock	tack
pack	luck	clock
rock	stack	truck
quack	buck	sack
knock	rack	stock
stuck	lock	yuck

ball	well	fill
sell	tall	smell
hill	fall	bell
hall	spell	drill
tell	pill	mall
spill	small	grill
wall	mill	shell

cat

hay

no match

tray

hat

play

rat

pay

bat

spray

mat

rake

Note to the teacher: Have a student sort the pictures and words; then have her match each word to its picture.

pin   sl**ide**

chin	ride	tin
side	fin	hide
win	bride	glide
stride	skin	grin
bin	tide	spin
pride	twin	wide

rain    **light**

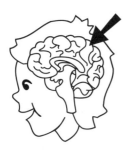

fight   chain   right

night   brain   train

Note to the teacher: Have a student sort the pictures and words; then have her match each word to its picture.

n**ail**	c**ake**	no match

snake	mail	snail
trail	bake	flame
lake	tail	rake

Note to the teacher: Have a student sort the pictures and words; then have her match each word to its picture.

dice

vine

nice	mine	slice
dine	shine	price
spice	mice	nine
whine	lice	spine
price	fine	rice
line	twice	pine

wh**ale**	g**ame**	wh**eat**
neat	came	male
tale	treat	same
frame	pale	beat
name	meat	cheat
sale	blame	scale
heat	stale	flame

ă as in  | **ĭ** as in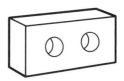

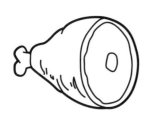  

Sorts of All Sorts • ©The Mailbox® Books • TEC61267

ŏ as in 	ŭ as in

 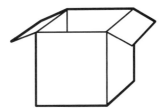 

 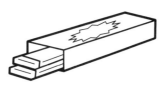 

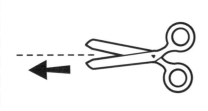 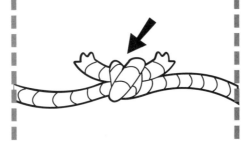 

ă as in  | ĭ as in

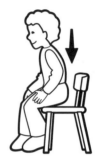

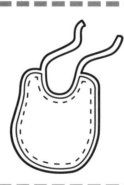

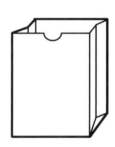

bib

map

bag

sit

fan

fin

Sorts of All Sorts • ©The Mailbox® Books • TEC61267

30 **Note to the teacher:** Have a student sort the pictures and words; then have her match each word to its picture.

ă as in	ŏ as in	ŭ as in

flag | bun | fox

rug | crab | pan

truck | pop | block

Note to the teacher: Have a student sort the pictures and words; then have her match each word to its picture.

31

ă as in 	ĭ as in

sat	lid	wig
fit	has	it
cab	his	nap
did	flag	clip
pat	drip	at
is	can	slam

ĕ as in 10	ŏ as in [log]	ŭ as in [rug]
yes	fun	rock
doll	on	red
bug	get	not
up	club	stop
men	dust	best
off	when	slug

ă as in	ĭ as in	ŭ as in
sang	lung	sing
stump	wink	blank
dunk	damp	junk
camp	sink	blimp
blink	dump	tank
sting	stamp	bump

ă as in    ā as in

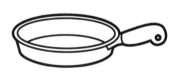      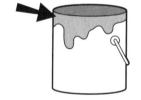

ŏ as in	ō as in	no match

pot	sock	hose
spoon	note	fox
globe	bone	mop

Note to the teacher: Have a student sort the pictures and words; then have her match each word to its picture.

ā as in 	**ī** as in 

ē as in	ō as in	no match
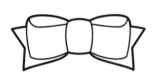		

goat	three	beak
bow	rope	dream
queen	moon	toast

Note to the teacher: Have a student sort the pictures and words; then have her match each word to its picture.

ā	ī	ū
tape	nine 9	mule

slide	mute	cube
plate	hive	bake
cage	fumes	smile

Note to the teacher: Have a student sort the pictures and words; then have her match each word to its picture.

ā rake	**ī** kite	**ō** hose
same	home	hide
robe	prize	gave
make	time	smoke
stone	came	shine
place	nice	vote
pile	throne	safe

ai p**ai**l	**ay** h**ay**	no match

paint | play | gray

lake | snail | train

tray | pray | mail

Note to the teacher: Have a student sort the pictures and words; then have her match each word to its picture.

ēē
wheel

ēa
beach

bean	seed	sleep
geese	freeze	bead
cream	teach	speed
street	east	clean
team	sheep	beak
queen	dream	teeth

$\overline{oa}$
soap

$\overline{ow}$
snow

slow	boat	grow
goat	know	road
toad	foam	crow
show	toast	own
soak	bowl	float
glow	throat	throw

ī child	igh light	ie pie
tie	right	find
wild	die	bright
fight	climb	fries
cries	knight	mind
tight	blind	lie
might	flies	kind

s 	t 	st

		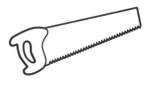

	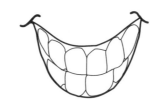	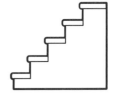

| **dr**  | **tr**  |

 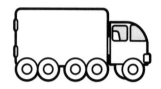 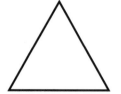

 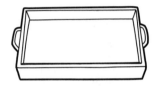 

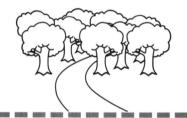  

 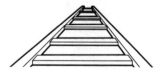 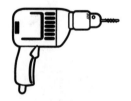

bl	cl	pl
		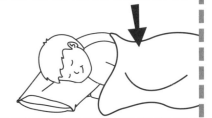
	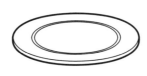	

	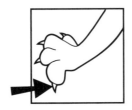	
	2 + 1 = 3	
The _____ is red. 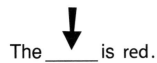		

sn 	sp 	sk 

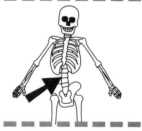		

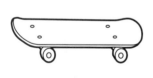		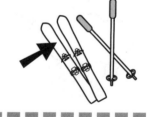
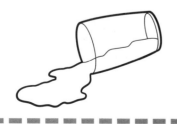	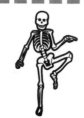	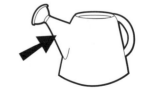

shell	**fish** 

  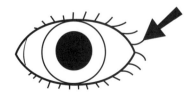

sh  | **th**

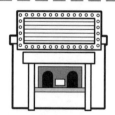 

Sort 45: Digraphs

ch	th 	wh 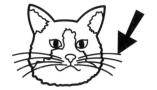
	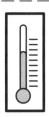	
30		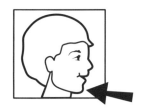

13		
		**3rd**

ă as in	ar as in	no match

track	shark	crab
star	stamp	yarn
bird	jar	mask

Note to the teacher: Have a student sort the pictures and words; then have her match each word to its picture.

herd	shirt	curl
girl	butter	hurt
fern	dirt	faster
church	stir	her
ladder	burn	first
third	sister	nurse
surf	turn	bird

Confusing Vowels

oo as in 🌙	oo as in 📖	no match ☹
(hook)	(foot)	(spoon)
(boot)	(stool)	(log)
(hood)	(box)	(zoo)
spoon	wood	box
foot	zoo	boot
stool	hood	hook

Sorts of All Sorts • ©The Mailbox® Books • TEC61267

Note to the teacher: Have a student sort the pictures and words; then have her match each word to its picture.

oi as in   **oy** as in

toy	enjoy	boil
oil	decoy	annoy
destroy	soil	foil
moist	joy	ahoy
soy	point	join
coil	ploy	avoid

Sort 50: Compound Words

compound words 🙂	not compound words ☹

snowman	**sea**food	**some**day
something	snowball	seashell
seashore	somewhere	seasick
snowsuit	snowfall	somehow
someone	seaside	snowstorm
snowplow	somebody	seaweed
seaport	sometime	snowflake

| contraction | not a contraction |

has not	I'm	I have
didn't	I will	do not
he is	hasn't	wasn't
did not	I've	have not
haven't	was not	he's
I'll	I am	don't

one	more than one

cap	bell	trucks
logs	grapes	dress
fox	glass	bees
cups	sock	gas
nuts	eggs	rats
desk	pins	grass

noun  | verb

sweep

frog

hand

kick

school

drink

log

clap

crab

fork

blow

skip

color	size	how many
green	purple	big
fat	several	red
blue	small	three
five	lots	little
large	orange	ten
few	long	yellow

6

10

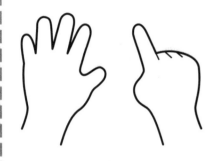

||||| |||||

six

ten

|||| |

7	**12**	no match
7 + 0 =	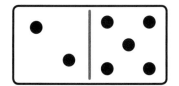	12 − 5 =
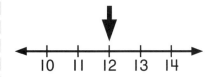	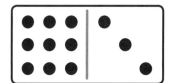	
8 − 4 =		seven
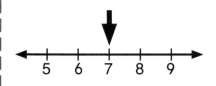		9 + 3 =
	twelve	
	7 + 5 =	12 − 0 =

less than 25	greater than 25

14	35	24
28	21	19
9	36	48
41	6	27
50	17	43
13	32	20

< 50	> 50

78	31	18
15	53	94
82	10	65
47	86	39
22	90	57
71	44	26

< 35	> 55	no match :(
16	85	29
74	38	70
27	63	15
33	30	77
42	59	23
19	61	98

7	9

☺ + ☺☺☺☺☺☺   ☺☺☺☺☺ + ☺☺☺☺   ☺☺☺☺ + ☺☺☺☺

☺ + ☺☺☺☺☺☺☺☺   ☺☺ + ☺☺☺☺☺☺   ☺☺☺☺☺☺ + ☺☺☺

☺☺☺☺ + ☺☺☺☺☺   ☺☺☺☺ + ☺☺☺   ☺☺☺ + ☺☺☺☺☺☺

☺☺☺☺☺ + ☺☺☺   ☺☺☺☺☺☺☺ + ☺☺   ☺☺☺☺☺ + ☺

6	8	10
4 + 4 =	3 + 3 =	2 + 6 =
8 + 2 =	0 + 8 =	5 + 1 =
2 + 4 =	4 + 6 =	3 + 5 =
1 + 9 =	7 + 1 =	6 + 4 =
6 + 0 =	5 + 5 =	1 + 5 =
5 + 3 =	4 + 2 =	3 + 7 =

9	12	13
5 + 4 =	6 + 7 =	9 + 4 =
7 + 5 =	9 + 3 =	3 + 6 =
5 + 8 =	4 + 9 =	8 + 5 =
8 + 4 =	6 + 3 =	5 + 7 =
9 + 0 =	7 + 6 =	8 + 1 =
4 + 8 =	2 + 7 =	6 + 6 =

10 or 11	14 or 15	16, 17, or 18
$5 + 6 =$	$8 + 7 =$	$9 + 9 =$
$9 + 8 =$	$7 + 7 =$	$2 + 8 =$
$8 + 3 =$	$9 + 1 =$	$8 + 8 =$
$9 + 7 =$	$5 + 9 =$	$9 + 6 =$
$7 + 3 =$	$8 + 9 =$	$7 + 8 =$
$6 + 8 =$	$7 + 9 =$	$4 + 7 =$

3	5

9 – 6

6 – 1

7 – 4

7 – 2

5 – 0

10 – 7

6 – 3

9 – 4

4 – 1

10 – 5

8 – 3

8 – 5

Subtraction

3	4	5
$10 - 5 =$	$6 - 1 =$	$9 - 6 =$
$7 - 3 =$	$5 - 2 =$	$11 - 6 =$
$9 - 5 =$	$12 - 7 =$	$8 - 4 =$
$6 - 3 =$	$10 - 6 =$	$12 - 8 =$
$8 - 5 =$	$9 - 4 =$	$7 - 4 =$
$11 - 7 =$	$10 - 7 =$	$8 - 3 =$

6	7	8
12 – 4 =	8 – 2 =	10 – 3 =
14 – 8 =	17 – 9 =	14 – 7 =
9 – 3 =	13 – 6 =	11 – 5 =
10 – 2 =	15 – 9 =	13 – 5 =
11 – 4 =	13 – 7 =	9 – 2 =
9 – 1 =	12 – 5 =	16 – 8 =

8	9	no match
16 − 8 =	15 − 6 =	14 − 6 =
14 − 5 =	12 − 4 =	18 − 9 =
15 − 7 =	14 − 9 =	10 − 2 =
13 − 4 =	17 − 8 =	11 − 3 =
11 − 2 =	12 − 3 =	15 − 8 =
17 − 9 =	13 − 5 =	16 − 7 =

5	7

$2 + 3 =$	$8 - 1 =$	$4 + 3 =$
$10 - 3 =$	$5 + 2 =$	$9 - 2 =$
$3 + 4 =$	$4 + 1 =$	$8 - 3 =$
$7 - 2 =$	$9 - 4 =$	$3 + 2 =$

4	5	7
$4 + 3 =$	$12 - 7 =$	$3 + 2 =$
$13 - 8 =$	$4 + 0 =$	$13 - 9 =$
$11 - 7 =$	$12 - 5 =$	$1 + 3 =$
$0 + 5 =$	$14 - 9 =$	$15 - 8 =$
$9 - 5 =$	$2 + 2 =$	$2 + 5 =$
$5 + 2 =$	$4 + 1 =$	$13 - 6 =$

6	8	9
$3 + 5 =$	$7 + 2 =$	$11 - 3 =$
$14 - 6 =$	$2 + 4 =$	$15 - 6 =$
$5 + 1 =$	$16 - 7 =$	$6 + 2 =$
$18 - 9 =$	$0 + 8 =$	$12 - 6 =$
$3 + 3 =$	$17 - 9 =$	$4 + 5 =$
$13 - 7 =$	$6 + 3 =$	$15 - 9 =$

7	9	no match
5 + 4 =	1 + 6 =	2 + 7 =
17 − 8 =	14 − 8 =	8 + 1 =
2 + 5 =	13 − 4 =	13 − 6 =
11 − 4 =	16 − 9 =	5 + 3 =
12 − 3 =	3 + 4 =	14 − 5 =
3 + 6 =	12 − 5 =	7 + 0 =

2 3 5	1 7 8	4 5 9
4 + 5 = 9	8 − 7 = 1	3 + 2 = 5
7 + 1 = 8	9 − 5 = 4	8 − 1 = 7
2 + 3 = 5	1 + 7 = 8	5 − 2 = 3
9 − 4 = 5	5 − 3 = 2	5 + 4 = 9

4 **3**	**3** **5**	**6** **3**
7	**8**	**9**
8 − 3 = 5	7 − 4 = 3	5 + 3 = 8
3 + 6 = 9	6 + 3 = 9	4 + 3 = 7
7 − 3 = 4	8 − 5 = 3	9 − 3 = 6
3 + 5 = 8	9 − 6 = 3	3 + 4 = 7

7 **5** **12**	**8** **5** **13**	**5** **9** **14**
$8 + 5 = 13$	$12 - 5 = 7$	$9 + 5 = 14$
$5 + 7 = 12$	$14 - 9 = 5$	$13 - 5 = 8$
$14 - 5 = 9$	$5 + 8 = 13$	$12 - 7 = 5$
$13 - 8 = 5$	$7 + 5 = 12$	$5 + 9 = 14$

6 8	8 7	9 6
14	15	15

15 − 7 = 8	6 + 8 = 14	15 − 9 = 6
6 + 9 = 15	15 − 6 = 9	15 − 8 = 7
8 + 6 = 14	7 + 8 = 15	14 − 6 = 8
9 + 6 = 15	14 − 8 = 6	8 + 7 = 15

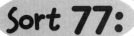

odd :• | even ••

odd	even
1, 3, 5, 7, 9...	0, 2, 4, 6, 8...

9	18	97
34	21	66
15	42	75
80	26	37
88	43	54
59	92	61

Sorts of All Sorts • ©The Mailbox® Books • TEC61267

Sort 79: Plane Shapes

no corners	3 corners	4 corners

Sort 80: Symmetry

symmetrical	not symmetrical

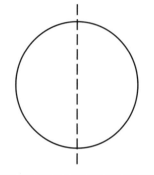 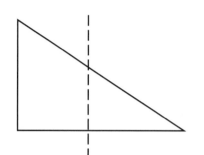 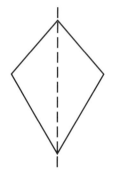

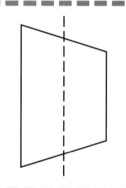 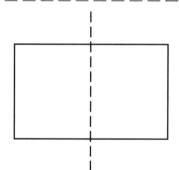 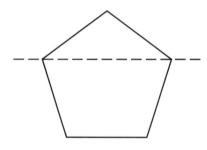

 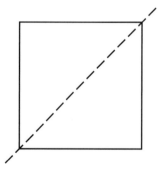 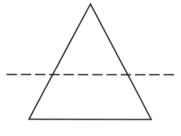

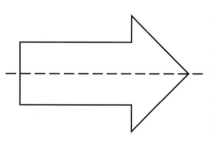 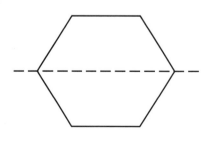 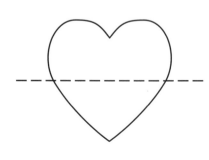

Sorts of All Sorts • ©The Mailbox® Books • TEC61267

Sort 81: Solid Figures

cone	cylinder	rectangular prism

Sort 82: Solid Figures

slide	stack	roll
Soup	C A B	(box)
Soup	C A B	(box)
Soup	Crackers	(orange)
(ball)	Crackers	(egg)

halves	thirds	fourths

$\frac{1}{2}$

$\frac{1}{3}$

$\frac{1}{4}$

$\frac{1}{2}$

$\frac{1}{3}$

$\frac{1}{4}$

$\dfrac{1}{2}$	$\dfrac{1}{3}$	$\dfrac{1}{4}$

longer than ▭	shorter than ▭
a ruler	a ruler

heavier than 	**lighter** than 

Sort 89: Measurement

more than 1  cup	**less** than 1  cup

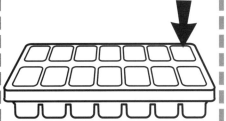

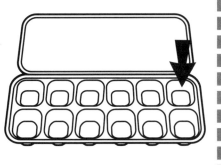

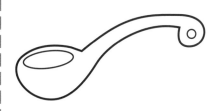

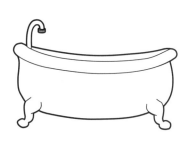

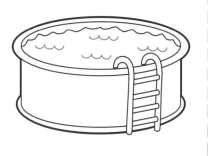

on the **hour**  | on the **half hour**

before 6:00	after 6:00

Note to the teacher: Have a student use a twelve-hour span of time to sort the pictures.

5¢	10¢	25¢

15¢	20¢	30¢

Money

35¢	45¢	50¢

Sorts of All Sorts • ©The Mailbox® Books • TEC61267

25¢	**50¢**	no match

summer	fall	winter

sweet 	salty 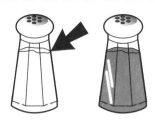

  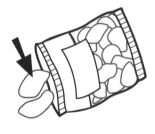

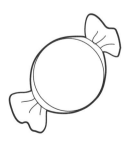  

soft  | hard

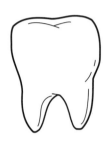

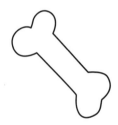

Sort 99: Sense of Sound

no sound	some sound	loud sound 

 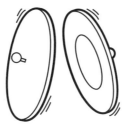 

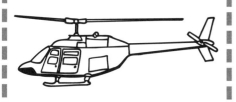 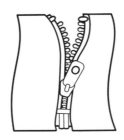 

living 	nonliving 

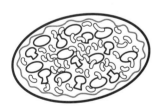

Sort 101: Animal Homes

animal    home

  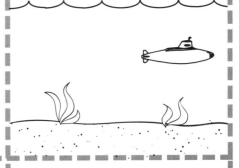

 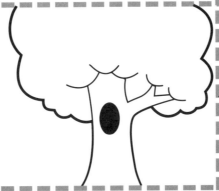 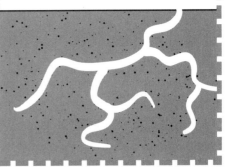

Sorts of All Sorts • ©The Mailbox® Books • TEC61267

Note to the teacher: Have a student sort the pictures; then have her match each animal to its home.

Sort 102: Animals

fur 	feathers 	scales

	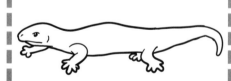	

Sort 103: Animals

forest animals	ocean animals

plant need 	not a plant need 

JUICE

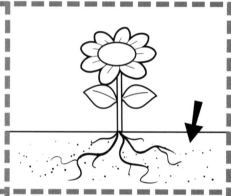

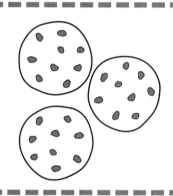

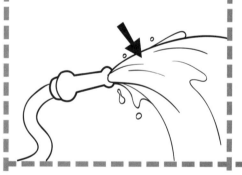

(air)

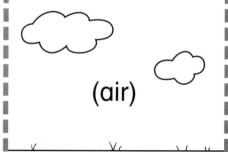

plant part	not a plant part

past 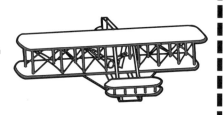 present

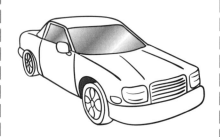 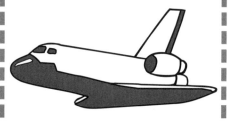 

0 wheels	2 wheels	4 wheels

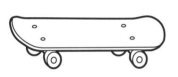  

  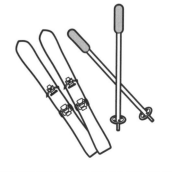

needs	wants

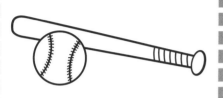  

goods	services

community goods and services 	**school** goods and services 

  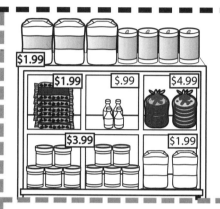

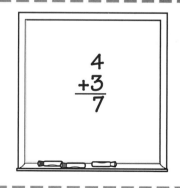  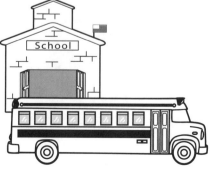

Sort 111: Geography

land	water

mountain

lake

peninsula

island

pond

desert

ocean

volcano

waterfall

river

valley

gulf

objects  | **symbols**

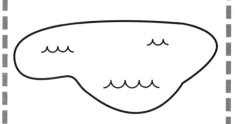

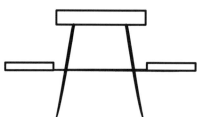

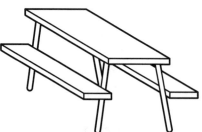

Sort 113: Environment

<table>
<tr>
<td>

good for the earth

</td>
<td>

bad for the earth

</td>
</tr>
</table>

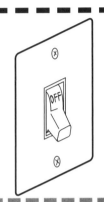

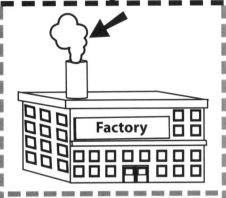

Factory

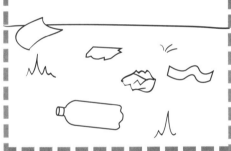

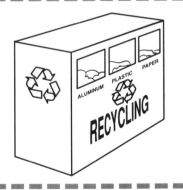

RECYCLING

ALUMINUM PLASTIC PAPER

reduce	reuse	recycle

Sorts of All Sorts • ©The Mailbox® Books • TEC61267

U.S. Symbol	Not a U.S. Symbol

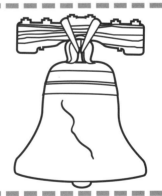

Programmable Sort:

Sorts of All Sorts • ©The Mailbox® Books • TEC61267

Name:

Sorts of All Sorts • ©The Mailbox® Books • TEC61267

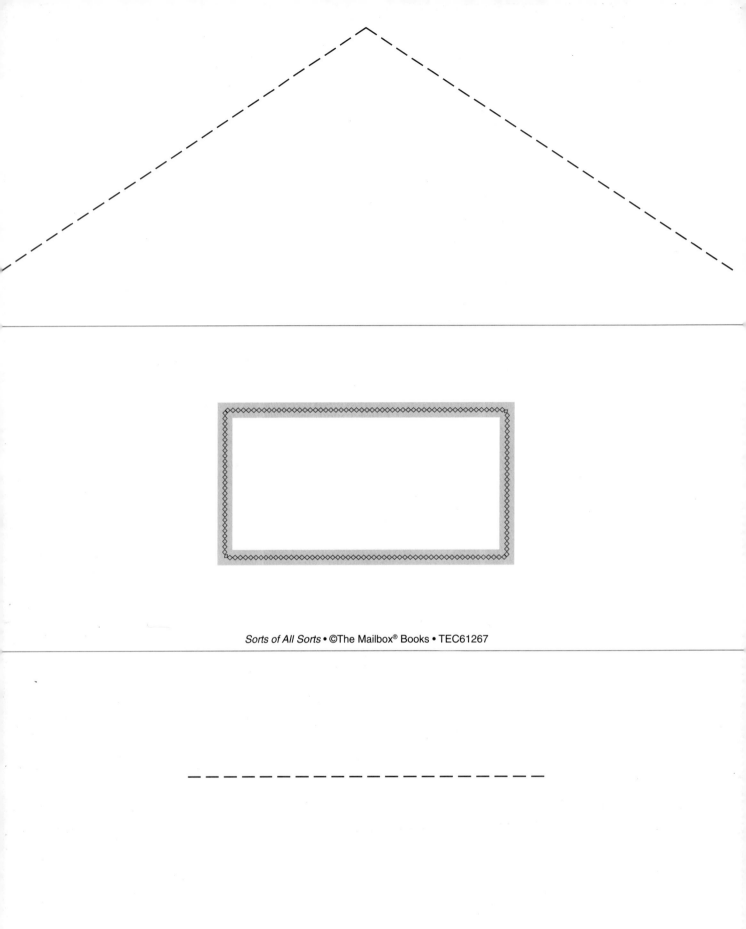

Sorts of All Sorts • ©The Mailbox® Books • TEC61267

Envelope Pattern: To make a storage envelope, copy this page and cut on the dotted lines. Fold along the bottom solid line (keeping the programming to the outside) and seal the left and right edges with glue. To close the envelope, fold the triangular flap down and tuck it into the slit.